SUMMARY OF END TIMES IN REAL TIME

Discern the Signs of the Times and Annihilate the Anti-Christ Agenda

JON HAMILL

JOLENE HAMILL

D DESTINY IMAGE

Destiny Image P.O. Box 310, Shippensburg, PA 17257-0310

This book and all other Destiny Image's books are available at Christian bookstores and distributors worldwide.

For Worldwide Distribution.

Reach us on the Internet: www.destinyimage.com.

ISBN 13 TP: 9798881504649

ISBN 13 eBook: 9798881504656

CONTENTS

INTRODUCTION

Introduction to the Summary of "End Times in Real Time"

Welcome to the journey through "End Times in Real Time," a pivotal exploration into the profound intersections of biblical prophecy, contemporary global events, and the individual's role in the unfolding divine narrative. This book, crafted in the crucible of today's most pressing challenges, seeks to awaken, equip, and empower believers for the role they are destined to play in this critical epoch of human history.

In "End Times in Real Time," the authors weave a compelling narrative that bridges the gap between ancient scriptural promises and modern-day fulfillments. Each chapter is meticulously designed to shed light on the spiritual dimensions governing current events, from geopolitical shifts and technological advancements to spiritual awakenings and moral dilemmas. The book does not merely describe these events; it prescribes a proactive stance for Christians everywhere, urging them to engage actively in shaping the future according to God's sovereign plan.

This summary aims to distill the essence of each chapter, providing readers with a concise yet comprehensive view of the book's core teachings and revelations. Whether you are a seasoned believer well-versed in eschatological studies or a newcomer seeking clarity in a world that seems increasingly complex and intertwined with spiritual significance, this summary offers valuable insights.

As you navigate through this summary, you will encounter key themes such as the role of prophecy in modern times, the identity and empowerment of the end-time church, and the strategic implications of our actions in the heavenly realms. Each section is crafted to not only inform but also to inspire a deeper engagement with the topics discussed, encouraging personal reflection and communal discussion.

"End Times in Real Time" is more than a book; it is a call to action. It challenges every reader to rise above the ordinary, to harness the potential embedded within the prophetic timelines, and to act with wisdom and courage in an era that demands nothing less. This summary captures the urgency and the transformative potential of its message, offering a beacon of understanding and empowerment for all who dare to partake in God's unfolding plan for the ages. As you turn these pages, prepare to be challenged, inspired, and equipped for such a time as this.

CHAPTER 1

A RELENTLESS VIGIL

Bible Verse

"Watch therefore, for you do not know what hour your Lord is coming" (Matthew 24:42 NKJV).

Introduction

"A Relentless Vigil" presents a contemporary examination of the end times, intertwined with personal anecdotes and a call to spiritual readiness. The author, a former journalism student turned spiritual revolutionary, discusses living and ministering in Washington DC, an epicenter of significant global conversations that seem to echo biblical prophecies about the end times.

Word of Wisdom

"End Times in Real Time is your summons to become spiritual revolutionaries, capable of moving yourself and your camp

beyond the undermining paralysis so many believers have succumbed to."

Main Theme

The chapter serves as a rallying cry for Christians to embrace their roles as vigilant watchmen during what could be the end times, encouraging a proactive engagement with God's word and an apostolic advancement through Jesus Christ.

Key Points

- The end times may feel more relevant today amid global crises and moral challenges.
- Understanding end times is not about fearing the apocalypse but preparing to overcome evil with spiritual insight and resilience.
- Personal experiences deeply influence one's spiritual journey and understanding of biblical truths.
- The concept of watchfulness is central to the Christian anticipation of Jesus' return.
- Idolatry and covenant-breaking are significant themes that believers must confront.
- Empowering God's justice and freedom in personal spheres is crucial for divine victory.

Key Themes

- The chapter emphasizes that every generation faces challenges that can be perceived as manifestations of the antichrist spirit, urging a robust spiritual response rather than an escape mentality. This historical continuity underscores the necessity for vigilance and spiritual courage in confronting present and future adversities.
- Through personal narratives, including a transformative personal encounter with Jesus, the author illustrates how profound spiritual experiences can anchor believers in truth and empower them through difficult times, offering an intimate glimpse into the transformative power of God's presence.
- The focus on apostolic and prophetic advancement highlights the importance of not only understanding biblical prophecies but actively engaging in fulfilling God's kingdom on earth, urging readers to shift from passivity to active participation in spiritual matters.
- The discussion about confronting idolatry and securing a covenant relationship with Jesus is portrayed as essential for navigating the end times effectively. This relationship is foundational to overcoming the antichrist influences within one's life and community.
- The author advocates for a real-time application of biblical strategies and divine insights that foster spiritual growth and

readiness, emphasizing consistent, prayerful engagement with God to discern His direction and secure His promises.

Conclusion

"A Relentless Vigil" is more than an analysis of the end times; it is a clarion call to Christians to rise as informed, proactive participants in God's unfolding plan. It challenges the reader to look beyond traditional eschatological teachings and explore deeper relational and spiritual dynamics at play, inviting a journey of active watchfulness and divine partnership.

CHAPTER 2

TWO BURNING LAMPS

Bible Verse

"Behold the bridegroom is coming; go out to meet
him!" (Matthew 25:6 NKJV)

Introduction

"Two Burning Lamps" draws a compelling
parallel between the historical midnight
ride of Paul Revere and the prophetic
call to prepare for Christ's return. This chapter
delves into the significance of being spiritually vigilant and ready, using historical and personal narratives to emphasize the urgency of the end times.

Word of Wisdom

*"The Lord is coming! Prepare the
way."*

Main Theme

This chapter is a clarion call to spiritual readiness, equipping believers to be forerunners of Christ's return, akin to Paul Revere's role in the American Revolution.

Key Points

- Prophetic warnings often go unnoticed until they become reality, as illustrated by the author's experience.
- Paul Revere's historical midnight ride is paralleled with a prophetic call to announce Christ's impending return.
- Cindy Jacobs's prophecy to the author redefined his ministry focus towards a more eschatological purpose.
- The COVID-19 pandemic and subsequent events of 2020 are interpreted as part of the prophetic "midnight crises" leading to the end times.
- The American Revolution is depicted as a spiritual precedent for breaking with tyranny and idolatry.
- The metaphor of the burning lamp in the Bible symbolizes covenant and divine presence.

Key Themes

- The role of prophets and spiritual leaders is crucial in times of complacency; their courage to speak on impending divine movements can awaken societies to spiritual realities. The author reflects on his own journey of recognizing the prophetic significance of his ministry in the context of end-time prophecies.

- The concept of "midnight crises" is explored through personal and national upheavals, particularly highlighting the transformative year of 2020 as a pivotal moment for the author's prophetic understanding and ministry direction.
- Historical analogies, like Paul Revere's ride and its impact on American independence, are used to illustrate the power of decisive, courageous action in times of crisis, drawing a line to spiritual action in preparing for Christ's return.
- The significance of covenant and the symbolic use of fire throughout biblical history emphasize God's persistent presence and guidance through trials, urging believers to maintain their covenant with Christ amidst modern challenges.
- The dual role of personal and communal preparation for the end times is underscored, suggesting that believers must not only prepare themselves spiritually but also act as beacons of preparation within their communities.

Conclusion

"Two Burning Lamps" serves as both a historical reflection and a prophetic urging, calling believers to recognize and respond to the signs of the times with the same urgency and resolve as the early

American patriots. It challenges readers to rise to the occasion as modern-day forerunners, preparing the way for Christ's return by being spiritually vigilant and active participants in God's unfolding plan.

CHAPTER 3

INAUGURATION

Bible Verse

"And I saw heaven opened, and behold, a white horse, and He who sat on it is called Faithful and True, and in righteousness He judges and makes war." (Revelation 19:11 NASB)

Introduction

"Inauguration" dives into the profound and timely insight that our generation stands at a critical intersection of biblical prophecy and current global events. With a focus on the implications of living in what may genuinely be the 'end times,' this chapter contemplates the spiritual and historical importance of being prepared for the return of Jesus Christ.

Word of Wisdom

"The Lord is coming! Prepare the way."

Main Theme

The chapter explores the thematic and prophetic connections between historical events like the American Revolution and spiritual watchfulness in contemporary times, urging believers to recognize and engage in the unfolding biblical narrative of the end times.

Key Points

- Biblical prophecies, such as the rebirth of Israel, indicate we are living in the end times.
- Recent global crises and political events align with biblical predictions of end-time scenarios.
- Spiritual vigilance and proactive engagement in God's kingdom are necessary responses to these signs.
- The parallels between historical figures like Paul Revere and modern-day believers highlight the ongoing call to readiness.
- The chapter uses the metaphor of 'inauguration' to discuss spiritual commissioning in the face of prophetic fulfillment.

Key Themes

- The rebirth of Israel in 1948 and subsequent global developments serve as clear markers that we are living in a biblically significant era. This reality requires a reassessment of our spiritual priorities and a renewed commitment to understanding and applying prophecy in our lives.

- The concept of spiritual watchfulness is not just about awaiting Christ's return but actively engaging in the spiritual battles and opportunities of our time. This involves recognizing the signs of the times, much like watchmen on a wall, and responding with informed, strategic prayer and action.

- Prophetic ministry and strategic prayer play crucial roles as believers navigate the end times. These spiritual disciplines enable believers to discern God's direction amid complex and often confusing global events, empowering the church to act with divine insight.

- The metaphor of 'inauguration' extends beyond political ceremonies to the spiritual commissioning of believers for the tasks ahead. As global events unfold in alignment with biblical prophecy, each believer is called to understand their unique role in God's redemptive plan, much like figures such as Paul Revere during the American Revolution.

- The chapter challenges readers to consider how the notion of 'end times in real time' applies personally and corporately. It encourages a lifestyle of preparedness and proactive engagement in the kingdom of God, fostering a mindset that blends watchfulness with active participation in unfolding divine events.

Conclusion

"Inauguration" serves as a spiritual rallying cry, likening believers to historical figures who stood at pivotal moments in their nations' histories. It calls for a deepened awareness of prophetic times, urging Christians to live in readiness and active engagement, knowing that our actions today are deeply entwined with biblical prophecies and the return of Christ. It's a call to step into our roles as modern-day forerunners, heralding the Kingdom of God with our lives and ministries.

CHAPTER 4

THE ARMAGEDDON CLOCK

Bible Verse

"I will betroth you to Me in righteousness and in justice, in lovingkindness and in compassion, and I will betroth you to Me in faithfulness. Then you will know the LORD." (Hosea 2:19-20 NASB)

Introduction

"The Armageddon Clock" delves into the profound symbolism of Armageddon and the Jezreel Valley in biblical prophecy, exploring how contemporary geopolitical and spiritual events are aligning with biblical end-times narratives, emphasizing the urgency and significance of these developments.

Word of Wisdom

"As it was in the days of the prophet so it is today. Armageddon is a backdrop for the spirit of Elijah."

. . .

Main Theme

This chapter connects historical biblical battles at Megiddo with modern tensions in the Middle East, particularly focusing on recent conflicts involving Israel and its implications for global prophecy. It underscores the urgency of recognizing and understanding the prophetic 'times' we live in, through the lens of Israel's central role in biblical prophecy.

Key Points

- Israel functions as God's prophetic clock for global events, shaping the spiritual narrative for Christians worldwide.
- Recent conflicts in Israel align strikingly with prophetic descriptions from the Bible, suggesting that modern events could be fulfilling ancient predictions.
- Prophetic songs and visions play a crucial role in understanding God's messages and timings, especially relating to Israel.
- The symbolism of the Jezreel Valley (Armageddon) ties directly to key biblical prophecies about the end times.
- The spiritual heritage and future implications of the region are deeply intertwined with the fate of nations globally.

Key Themes

- **Prophetic Centrality of Israel**: Israel's geopolitical conflicts are not just regional but serve as a barometer for the prophetic timeline concerning end times. The rebirth of Israel and subsequent regional conflicts underscore its biblical role as a pivotal arena for prophetic fulfillment.

- **Symbolic Significance of Armageddon**: Armageddon, or Tel Megiddo, is more than a historical site; it's a prophetic symbol deeply embedded in Christian eschatology. The valley has been a site of numerous biblical battles and is prophesied to be the staging ground for the final battle between good and evil.

- **Interpretation of Prophetic Signs**: Understanding the times through prophetic signs, such as celestial events and geopolitical shifts, requires a deep engagement with Scripture and spiritual discernment. These signs are often pointers to larger, divine scripts unfolding in real-time.

- **Role of Prophetic Ministry in Modern Times**: The function of prophetic ministry today is to alert and prepare the global church for the unfolding of end-time events. This involves interpreting current events through the lens of Scripture and encouraging vigilance and readiness among believers.

- **Implications of Modern Events for Biblical Prophecy**: The chapter suggests that events like the conflict between Israel and Hamas may be precursors to the ultimate prophetic battle predicted in Revelation. Such events prompt believers to reflect on their spiritual readiness and the global implications of these conflicts.

Conclusion

"The Armageddon Clock" challenges believers to consider the prophetic significance of current events, especially those involving Israel, as indicators of the biblical end times. It calls for a renewed commitment to understanding and engaging with prophecy, emphasizing the role of Israel as God's prophetic clock and the need for spiritual preparedness in anticipation of Christ's return.

CHAPTER 5

SPIRIT OF ELIJAH

Bible Verse

"As the Lord God of Israel lives, before whom I stand, there shall not be dew nor rain these years, except at my word!" (1 Kings 17:1 NKJV)

Introduction

In "Spirit of Elijah," the authors recount their prophetic journey to Israel, emphasizing the significance of the Elijah mantle in biblical and contemporary contexts. They explore the transformative power of this prophetic anointing, which is crucial for spiritual turnaround and restoration in today's turbulent times.

Word of Wisdom

"What if picking up the mantle is actually not about you in the least?"

Main Theme

This chapter focuses on the profound spiritual significance of the mantle of Elijah, exploring its historical roots and its current necessity for catalyzing spiritual renewal and covenant restoration within the Body of Christ.

Key Points

- The mantle of Elijah symbolizes a powerful spiritual anointing for turning hearts back to God and restoring broken relationships.
- This mantle was symbolically picked up by the authors in Israel, signifying a global shift in the prophetic movement.
- The Spirit of Elijah is essential for confronting and overturning modern-day idolatries and societal corruption.
- Elijah's mantle is about covenant restoration, crucial for both personal and communal revival.
- The anointing associated with Elijah is meant to empower believers to enact divine justice and mercy in their communities.

Key Themes

- **Prophetic Action and Covenant Renewal**: The act of picking up Elijah's mantle near the Jordan River is portrayed as a covenantal act, aimed at renewing the

Church's commitment to God's purposes and preparing it for end-time challenges. This prophetic symbolism is deeply tied to the biblical story of Elijah and Elisha, underscoring the mantle's role in spiritual succession and empowerment.

- **Transformation Through Consecration**: The chapter stresses the necessity of personal and communal consecration to receive and wield the mantle effectively. Just as Gideon's victory was predicated on his rejection of Baal, modern believers are called to forsake spiritual compromise to embrace God's call fully.

- **Intercessory Prayer and Prophetic Declaration**: The authors emphasize the role of intercessory prayer and prophetic declaration in activating the mantle's power. They recount how their prayers and prophetic acts in Israel were aligned with global shifts in the spiritual realm, suggesting that such actions can have far-reaching effects.

- **Challenges of Spiritual Leadership**: The narrative explores the weight of spiritual leadership and the humility required to wield Elijah's mantle effectively. It challenges readers to consider the broader impact of their spiritual gifts, not for personal gain but for communal restoration and revival.

- **Readiness for Spiritual Warfare**: By invoking the spirit and power of Elijah, the authors underscore the readiness needed for the spiritual battles that define our times. They draw parallels between biblical times and today, suggesting that just as Elijah combated the corrupt leadership of Ahab and Jezebel, believers today are called to confront and overcome modern manifestations of these spirits.

Conclusion

"Spirit of Elijah" calls for a deep, transformative engagement with the prophetic legacy of Elijah, urging believers to actively seek and uphold a high standard of spiritual purity and power. It presents the Elijah mantle not just as a symbol of prophetic authority, but as a vital tool for spiritual warfare and societal transformation, essential for navigating the complexities of the end times.

CHAPTER 6
SOUNDING FORTH THE TRUMPET

Bible Verse

"He is sounding forth the trumpet that shall never call retreat; He is sifting out the hearts of men before His judgment seat..." —"Battle Hymn of the Republic"

Introduction

In "Sounding Forth the Trumpet," the authors recount their transformative journey in Israel, culminating in a profound experience at Yad Vashem, Israel's Holocaust Memorial. The narrative connects the historical significance of the Holocaust with contemporary issues of anti-semitism and spiritual warfare.

Word of Wisdom

"The enemy desperately wants our generation to forget the Holocaust, to ignore it altogether, even while laying the

groundwork for a new holocaust in our day."

Main Theme

This chapter explores the prophetic significance of sounding the shofar (trumpet) as a call to remembrance and action against rising antisemitism and spiritual complacency in today's world.

Key Points

- The shofar sounded at Yad Vashem symbolized a call to remember the Holocaust and fight against antisemitism.
- Prophetic warnings of terrorism and political strife highlighted the importance of vigilance and prayer.
- The Holocaust's history serves as a sobering reminder of the consequences of unchecked hatred and antisemitism.
- The Spirit of Elijah Tour was marked by significant prophetic experiences, emphasizing the urgency of God's message for the present times.
- Antisemitism is portrayed as a persistent evil that requires constant vigilance and resistance from both Jews and Christians.

Key Themes

- **Historical and Prophetic Continuity**: The visit to Yad Vashem and the sounding of the shofar underscored a historical and spiritual continuity that binds past atrocities with current events. The chapter illustrates how remembering the Holocaust is essential not only for honoring the past but for guarding against future atrocities.
- **The Role of the Shofar in Prophetic Acts**: The act of sounding the shofar at significant moments throughout the tour serves as a powerful symbol of awakening and alert. It is depicted as a divine tool for rallying God's people against spiritual and physical threats.
- **Connection Between Antisemitism and Prophetic Warnings**: The chapter connects the dots between historical antisemitism, such as the Holocaust, and its modern resurgence, emphasizing the prophetic duty to stand against such evils. It suggests that the failure to remember and learn from history could lead to repeated tragedies.
- **Impact of Spiritual Vigilance on Societal Events**: The narrative highlights the critical role of spiritual vigilance and prophetic responsiveness in influencing societal events and shaping historical outcomes. The authors call for a renewed commitment to this vigilance as a defense against spiritual and societal decay.
- **Unity in the Face of Antisemitism**: The collective response of the tour group,

declaring solidarity with the Jewish people, exemplifies the potential for unity in combating antisemitism. This unity is portrayed as a spiritual and moral imperative that transcends cultural and religious boundaries.

Conclusion

"Sounding Forth the Trumpet" serves as a clarion call to remember the lessons of the past, to stand firm against the resurgence of antisemitism, and to engage in spiritual warfare with the urgency and power that the times demand. It challenges readers to rise to the occasion, equipped with the prophetic insight and spiritual tools necessary to influence the world for the better.

CHAPTER 7

COME UP HIGHER—
EXITING THE X

Bible Verse

"Gather My godly ones to Me, those who have made a covenant with Me by sacrifice" (Psalm 50:5 NASB).

Introduction

In "Come Up Higher—Exiting the X," the author discusses the intensifying spiritual and societal challenges in the U.S. and Israel, emphasizing the need for a higher spiritual response amidst these crises.

Word of Wisdom

"Remember what you've learned. Armageddon is a backdrop for the spirit and power of Elijah. The best is yet to come!"

Main Theme

The chapter explores the prophetic significance of overcoming trials through spiritual elevation and the importance of responding to God's call to rise above the crises defining the modern world.

Key Points

• The shofar gifted at Yad Vashem symbolized a call to vigilance against rising global antisemitism.

• Prophetic warnings highlight the urgency of spiritual readiness and the necessity to ascend spiritually.

• Disturbing events are seen as signs of the times, demanding a higher level of spiritual engagement.

• The exposure of sin within the church emphasizes the need for purity and reformation among believers.

• The author uses personal experiences and prophetic insights to call for repentance and a return to covenant faithfulness.

Key Themes

- **Prophetic Alarms and Urgency**: The chapter stresses the importance of heeding prophetic warnings, particularly those sounding alarms about societal and spiritual deterioration. These alarms are not just wake-up calls but directives for proactive spiritual action.
- **Necessity for Spiritual Elevation**: In response to escalating crises, there is a

profound need for believers to "come up higher." This involves engaging more deeply in spiritual disciplines, accessing heavenly perspectives, and responding with increased moral clarity.

- **Impact of Sin on Collective Integrity**: The revelation of sin within leadership highlights the catastrophic impact on the community's spiritual health. This serves as a somber reminder that the integrity of the community is often compromised from within, not just from external pressures.

- **Historical and Eschatological Context**: The author places recent events within a broader historical and eschatological context, suggesting that current challenges are part of a cyclical pattern of divine testing and judgment, leading to an ultimate purification and restoration.

- **Call to Covenant Faithfulness**: The narrative calls for a return to covenant faithfulness, urging readers to recommit to God's commands and promises. This recommitment is framed as essential for navigating the end times with God's favor and protection.

Conclusion

"Come Up Higher—Exiting the X" implores readers to rise above the tumult of the times by deepening their spiritual commitment and adhering more closely to God's statutes. It underscores the necessity of maintaining vigilance, purity, and a prophetic voice in an era of profound moral and spiritual challenges. The chapter serves as a clarion call for believers to elevate their lives and influence through heightened devotion and obedience to God.

CHAPTER 8

TESHUVAH

Bible Verse
"Seek the Lord while He may be found; call upon Him while He is near" (Isaiah 55:6 NASB).

Introduction

In the chapter "Teshuvah," the author delves into the concept of repentance and its crucial role in the individual and collective spiritual journey, particularly within the context of prophetic movements and leadership crises.

Word of Wisdom

"Purity lit a candle and, through tears, called for repentance."

Main Theme

The chapter emphasizes the transformative power of repentance (Teshuvah) in mending personal and communal relationships with God, underpinning it with personal prophetic experiences and biblical narratives to illustrate its profound necessity and urgency.

Key Points

• The concept of Teshuvah, which means repentance, is central to improving our spiritual lives and communities.

• Repentance involves a deep, personal introspection and a turning back to God's path.

• True repentance can influence not only individuals but also collective entities like churches and nations.

• The Jewish High Holy Days, particularly Rosh Hashanah and Yom Kippur, embody the spirit of Teshuvah, emphasizing introspection and reconciliation.

• The author's personal prophetic experiences underscore the need for purity and repentance within the leadership to avert spiritual and moral crises.

Key Themes

• **Prophetic Insight and Accountability**: The chapter discusses the role of prophetic insight in holding leaders accountable, addressing why some leaders fail to see or act upon impending moral failings within movements. The prophetic is not just about foretelling events but involves steering communities towards righteousness and repentance.

- **Repentance as Divine Mandate**: Teshuvah is presented not just as a recommendation but as a divine mandate, crucial for spiritual renewal and preventing judgment. The author uses scriptural references to highlight how repentance can lead to divine mercy and a refreshing presence from the Lord.
- **Historical and Ritual Importance of Teshuvah**: The chapter details the historical and ritual significance of Teshuvah during the Jewish High Holy Days, illustrating how these practices can model for Christians the importance of dedicated times of repentance and reflection.
- **Impact of Leadership on Community**: It discusses the profound impact leaders have on their communities and how their actions can lead to either blessing or destruction. The narrative encourages leaders to embrace repentance and humility to safeguard their followers.
- **Personal and Communal Actions for Repentance**: Steps for engaging in Teshuvah are outlined, which include self-examination, seeking forgiveness, forgiving others, and making amends. These actions are foundational for healing and restoring relationships both with God and within communities.

Conclusion

"Teshuvah" calls for a heartfelt return to God through repentance, emphasizing its necessity at both personal and communal levels. The chapter challenges individuals and leaders alike to introspect, acknowledge their shortcomings, and seek God's forgiveness to usher in a period of spiritual renewal and divine favor. It underscores the urgency of living in alignment with God's will through continual repentance and realignment with divine principles.

CHAPTER 9

RESCUING YOUR LAMPSTAND

Bible Verse

"Set me as a seal upon your heart, as a seal upon your arm; for love is as strong as death, jealousy as cruel as the grave; Its flames are flames of fire, a most vehement flame" (Song of Songs 8:6 NKJV).

Introduction

In "Rescuing Your Lampstand," the author explores the spiritual concept of maintaining one's passion and devotion to God, likening it to keeping a lampstand lit amidst the winds of trials, neglect, and resistance.

Word of Wisdom

"Jesus, I'm breaking up with You."

Main Theme

This chapter discusses the vital importance of rekindling one's first love with God, characterized by passion and devotion, and offers practical steps to ignite this spiritual fervor once again.

Key Points

• The lampstand symbolizes one's devotion and passion for God, which can dim over time due to various challenges.

• Jesus is actively interested in helping believers restore their spiritual fervor and maintain their 'lampstands.'

• Personal experiences and biblical narratives are used to illustrate the process of losing and reigniting passion for God.

• The chapter includes practical steps to recover one's spiritual passion, emphasizing honesty, covenant renewal, and rediscovering Jesus.

• Jolene's personal story of breaking up with Jesus provides a relatable example of struggling with and rediscovering first love.

Key Themes

- **Understanding the Lampstand**: The lampstand is a biblical metaphor for a believer's passion and visible devotion to God. The author emphasizes that without active maintenance, the light of our lampstand can dim, which necessitates intentional actions to keep it burning brightly.

- **Spiritual Renewal Through Honesty**: One of the first steps to renewing one's spiritual fervor is to engage in honest dialogue with God about one's feelings and struggles. This transparency is pivotal for addressing the root causes of spiritual malaise and for re-establishing a heartfelt connection with God.
- **Practical Steps for Reigniting Passion**: The author provides specific actions such as welcoming God's love, renewing covenant vows, and engaging in spiritual practices that were foundational during the early stages of one's faith journey. These actions help to restore the brightness of one's spiritual life and deepen one's relationship with God.
- **The Role of Challenges in Spiritual Growth**: The narrative acknowledges that believers often face significant challenges that can dampen their spiritual enthusiasm. However, these challenges also present opportunities for growth and deeper reliance on God's strength and provision.
- **Encouragement to Actively Pursue God**: The chapter encourages readers to actively pursue God, likening believers to the Maccabees who fought to reclaim and rededicate the Temple. This metaphor serves as a powerful call to action for believers to fight against complacency and rekindle their spiritual commitment.

Conclusion

"Rescuing Your Lampstand" calls for a heartfelt examination and revival of one's spiritual passion. It emphasizes that maintaining a vibrant relationship with God requires continuous effort, akin to tending a flame. Through practical advice and encouraging words, the author implores readers to rediscover their first love for God, ensuring that their spiritual lampstands remain bright and burning in the midst of end times.

CHAPTER 10

COME UP HIGHER—
BEFORE HIS FACE

Bible Verse

"Come up here, and I will show things which must [shortly] take place..." (Revelation 4:1 NKJV).

Introduction

"Come Up Higher—Before His Face" invites readers into a deeper, transformative engagement with God, using the imagery of ascending to a higher spiritual plane to illustrate the process of receiving divine revelation and understanding God's will in real time.

Word of Wisdom

"God isn't future, GOD IS NOW."

Main Theme

The chapter emphasizes the importance of drawing nearer to God to receive end-times revelation and to understand His immediate presence and ongoing work in our lives and the world.

Key Points

• Spiritual ascent is linked to a deeper revelation of God's purposes and plans.

• True apostolic calling involves first coming into God's presence before being sent out.

• The authority to act on God's behalf comes from intimate encounters with Him.

• Prophets and spiritual leaders have historically derived their authority from time spent in God's council.

• The chapter argues for a balance between being in God's presence and acting out His commands in the world.

Key Themes

• **Direct Encounter with Divine Presence**: The author describes the transformative power of being called into God's presence, where believers receive not only commissioning but also the divine vision necessary to impact the world effectively. This engagement is foundational for effective spiritual leadership and ministry.

- **Apostolic Model of Ministry**: The model of being sent out 'before His face' emphasizes that effective ministry begins with a direct, personal encounter with Christ. This initial encounter equips believers with the clarity and authority needed to carry out God's work on earth.
- **Elijah's Example of Divine Authority**: Through the example of Elijah, the author illustrates how prophets gain authority and directive from their time spent in the divine council. This proximity to God's presence allowed Elijah to enact significant changes in Israel, demonstrating the practical impact of divine communion.
- **Implications for Contemporary Believers**: Readers are encouraged to seek personal revelatory experiences with God as a normal part of Christian life. This relationship is portrayed as dynamic and essential for understanding and participating in God's actions in today's world.
- **Authority Through Covenant and Commission**: The chapter links spiritual authority directly to covenant relationships with God, stressing that seats of spiritual authority are established and sustained through ongoing fidelity to God's covenant and commands.

Conclusion

"Come Up Higher—Before His Face" challenges believers to deepen their relational ties with God to understand His will and enact His plans on earth. It suggests that direct encounters with God not only transform individuals but also empower them to effect meaningful change in their environments, fulfilling God's purposes in these pivotal times.

CHAPTER 11

THE MIDNIGHT RIDERS: FORERUNNER MINISTRY IN THE END TIMES

Bible Verse

"Behold, I send My messenger, and he will prepare the way before Me." - Malachi 3:1 NKJV

Introduction

The chapter draws on historical and biblical narratives of vigilant watchfulness and proactive engagement in God's plans, illustrating the critical role of forerunners in the end times through the lens of Paul Revere's midnight ride and Gideon's strategic battle preparations.

Word of Wisdom

"Heaven is ready to ride!"

Main Theme

This chapter explores the concept of forerunner ministries in the end times, emphasizing the need for spiritual vigilance, prophetic insight, and readiness to act upon divine revelation to navigate and influence pivotal historical changes.

Key Points

• Historical and spiritual parallels are drawn between Paul Revere's ride and the vigilant role of modern spiritual forerunners.

• The necessity of real-time, prophetic intelligence in spiritual warfare is emphasized.

• Modern-day believers are likened to Gideon's warriors, called to strategic, covert spiritual operations.

• Prophetic experiences are pivotal in guiding believers through end-time crises.

• The chapter underscores the urgency of spiritual readiness for impending divine moves.

• Forerunners are depicted as crucial in preparing the spiritual landscape for Christ's return.

Key Themes

• **Strategic Spiritual Warfare**: The chapter illustrates how God uses spiritually attuned individuals to act as modern-day Paul Reveres, who discern and disseminate divine strategies against impending spiritual and worldly crises. This role is crucial in preventing spiritual slumber and promoting a vigilant, battle-ready stance among believers.

- **Prophetic Insight and Real-Time Revelation**: Emphasizing the importance of receiving and acting on real-time revelations from God, the text describes how such insights equip believers to effectively engage in spiritual warfare and societal transformation, mirroring the historical impact of intelligence used during revolutionary wars.

- **The Role of Forerunners in Divine Strategy**: Forerunners are depicted as essential to God's strategic deployment for His end-time plans, acting under direct divine commission to prepare the way for significant spiritual shifts and movements, much like the scouts in ancient battles.

- **Importance of Spiritual Preparedness**: Drawing parallels to the wise virgins in Matthew 25, the narrative stresses the necessity for believers to maintain spiritual vigilance and preparedness, ensuring they are ready to act when God moves.

- **Covenant and Divine Commissioning**: The chapter connects the effectiveness of forerunners to their covenant relationship with God, highlighting that true spiritual authority to act on God's behalf springs from a place of covenantal fidelity and divine commissioning.

Conclusion

"The Midnight Riders: Forerunner Ministry in the End Times" calls believers to rise to the occasion as vigilant, proactive agents of God's end-time plans. By equipping themselves with prophetic insight and readiness, they prepare the spiritual terrain for significant divine movements, ensuring they are part of the vanguard that heralds Christ's imminent return.

CHAPTER 12

THE HARVEST WARS: OVERCOMING END-TIME IDOLATRY

Bible Verse

"Yet even now," declares the Lord, "return to me with all your heart, with fasting, with weeping, and with mourning; and rend your hearts and not your garments." - Joel 2:12 ESV

Introduction

In this chapter, the focus shifts to the spiritual battlegrounds of modern times, drawing parallels to the ancient confrontations between Elijah and the corrupt rulers Ahab and Jezebel, illustrating a continual struggle against the forces of idolatry that seeks to dominate the spiritual harvests of nations.

Word of Wisdom

"The third great awakening is a great return, where multitudes disengage from

Jezebel's table and return to the Table of the Lord."

Main Theme

This chapter explores the enduring conflict between godly righteousness and idolatrous corruption, termed as "Harvest Wars," where believers are called to reclaim the spiritual territory through vigilance, prayer, and divine intervention, reflecting the epic struggles of biblical prophets.

Key Points

• Elijah's historic battle against Ahab and Jezebel mirrors today's spiritual warfare over the hearts and lands of people.

• Jezebel's modern counterparts corrupt societies through idolatry, much like the ancient queen did in Israel.

• The Harvest Wars are described as a fight for spiritual dominion and the souls of nations.

• Believers are called to engage actively in reclaiming their spiritual heritage and authority.

• The chapter outlines strategies for overcoming idolatry through prayer, repentance, and prophetic action.

• It emphasizes the restoration of divine order and covenant through the active participation of God's people.

Key Themes

- **Elijah's Prophetic Model of Confrontation**: The chapter uses Elijah's confrontation with Ahab and Jezebel as a template for addressing modern-day idolatry, emphasizing that the same spirit of courage and divine backing is necessary to challenge and overthrow the pervasive influence of corruption and moral decay in society.

- **The Modern Manifestation of Jezebel**: Jezebel's spirit is depicted as a pervasive force in contemporary culture, manipulating media, politics, and social norms to promote idolatry and immorality. The text calls for believers to recognize and resist this influence through strategic spiritual warfare and societal engagement.

- **Strategic Prayer and Prophetic Declaration**: Highlighting the power of prophetic declarations and prayer, the chapter encourages believers to utilize these tools to enforce divine verdicts against spiritual adversaries, thereby reclaiming territories and destinies for God's Kingdom.

- **Restoration Through Repentance and Return**: It advocates for a collective return to covenantal fidelity, where communities and nations forsake idolatrous practices to embrace the purity and authority of biblical standards, facilitated by heartfelt repentance and renewal.

- **Covenant Reclamation and Divine Justice**: The narrative asserts that God's people can invoke divine justice against idolatrous oppressions by appealing to Heaven's court, ensuring that covenants with demonic forces are annulled and God's righteous order is reinstated in governance and societal structures.

Conclusion

"The Harvest Wars: Overcoming End-Time Idolatry" challenges readers to rise in the spirit of Elijah and reclaim the spiritual heritage of their lands from the grip of modern-day Jezebels. Through repentance, prophetic warfare, and unwavering faith, believers are equipped to win the crucial battles for their generations and restore the sanctity of their divine covenant with God.

CHAPTER 13

END-TIMES TREACHERY AND TRICKERY

Bible Verse

"Do not believe every spirit, but test the spirits to see whether they are from God, for many false prophets have gone out into the world." - 1 John 4:1 ESV

Introduction

This chapter explores the pervasive themes of treachery and trickery in contemporary society, drawing from historical, political, and biblical perspectives to illustrate how these deceitful practices manifest in various spheres, including religion and governance.

Word of Wisdom

"Treachery and Trickery—two of the enemy's greatest strategies in the end times."

Main Theme

Focusing on the dual threats of treachery and trickery, this chapter delves into their impact on personal, societal, and spiritual levels, emphasizing the need for heightened discernment and proactive spiritual warfare to counter these end-time strategies.

Key Points

• The chapter opens with cultural observations linking modern celebrations like Halloween to broader themes of evil and deception.

• It recounts a specific political incident to illustrate how treachery can be masked by public actions.

• A significant portion discusses a personal dream that emphasized the rise of a false church and the need for discernment.

• The biblical context of treachery and trickery is explored through scriptural references and interpretations.

• Practical guidance on discerning and opposing deceit in various forms is provided.

• Communion is proposed as a spiritual act to expose and counter betrayal.

Key Themes

- **Cultural Reflections on Deception**:
The chapter begins by juxtaposing playful cultural traditions against the serious undertones of deceit they can represent, suggesting that even in seemingly innocent settings, the seeds of trickery can be sown, influencing societal norms and individual behaviors.
- **Personal and Political Deception**:
Using both a personal anecdote involving a political leader and a recounting of a significant dream, the chapter illustrates how deception infiltrates both the highest levels of government and personal spiritual experiences, necessitating a vigilant and discerning response.
- **Biblical Insights on Discernment**:
Scriptural references are used to underscore the importance of testing spirits and teachings against the truth of God's Word, with specific emphasis on avoiding the pitfalls of false prophets and teachings that lead away from Christ.
- **Practical Steps for Discerning Truth**:
The narrative provides concrete advice for developing spiritual discernment, including the need to remain spiritually attuned and proactive in identifying and combating deceit in all areas of life.
- **Communion as a Tool for Exposure**:
The act of taking communion is highlighted not only as a means of fellowship with Christ but also as a prophetic act to expose and pray against

the spiritual treachery within the church and society.

Conclusion

"End-Times Treachery and Trickery" challenges readers to elevate their spiritual vigilance and discernment as key defenses against the increasing deception of the times. By embracing biblical wisdom and engaging in proactive spiritual practices, believers are equipped to identify and overcome the subtle yet dangerous influences of treachery and trickery that pervade modern life.

CHAPTER 14

TURN THE STORM: END-TIME PERIL, END-TIME GLORY

Bible Verse

"Run in such a way that you may win." - 1 Corinthians 9:24 NASB

Introduction

This chapter weaves the profound challenges of end-time events with the transcendent glory that believers are called to manifest. It explores the intertwining of personal, national, and global crises with God's overarching plan for spiritual awakening and transformation.

Word of Wisdom

"Storms are coming that you cannot avert. But you CAN TURN THE STORM so the winds blow you, and the waves take you in the right direction."

Main Theme

The chapter emphasizes the dual reality of increasing global turbulence and the believer's role as an overcomer equipped to navigate and transform these challenges through divine empowerment.

Key Points

• The book's completion aligns symbolically with significant Jewish holidays, emphasizing a time of reflection and repentance.

• Personal and global crises are portrayed as opportunities for believers to demonstrate God's power.

• The narrative underscores the importance of spiritual preparation and the embracing of one's divine calling.

• It details the strategic significance of Israel and the U.S. in global politics and spiritual warfare.

• The chapter calls for active engagement in spiritual warfare and the prophetic intercession to shape the future.

Key Themes

- **Prophetic Timing and Alignment**: The chapter links significant prophetic dates and events, suggesting that God's people are entering a crucial phase where their actions align with divine timings, such as Rosh Hashanah and Yom Kippur, which are symbolic of repentance and atonement.

- **The Overcomer's Identity**: Readers are encouraged to view themselves as overcomers, a central theme where spiritual growth through trials is paralleled with training like elite warriors, emphasizing that overcoming is not just about survival but about excelling in God's assignments.
- **Strategic Spiritual Warfare**: The complexities of global events, including tensions between nations like the U.S., Israel, and Iran, are presented not just as political issues but as spiritual battlegrounds where believers must engage through informed, strategic prayer.
- **Divine Empowerment in Crises**: Drawing parallels between biblical figures like Elijah and modern-day believers, the narrative encourages embracing 'wilderness seasons' as times of divine training for higher purposes, preparing them to handle greater anointings and responsibilities.
- **Vision of God's Glory**: A powerful depiction of God's glory as described in the visions of Ezekiel, emphasizing that the ultimate purpose of believers is to facilitate the manifestation of this glory on earth through their lives and actions.

Conclusion

"Turn the Storm: End-Time Peril, End-Time Glory" serves as a clarion call for believers to rise and embody their divine destinies as agents of change in tumultuous times. It challenges readers to not only expect end-time challenges but to actively engage in turning these situations for God's glory through spiritual maturity and prophetic action. This chapter insists that the epoch known as the end times, though fraught with peril, is destined to crescendo in divine glory, affirming the believer's role in heralding this supernatural transformation.

www.ingramcontent.com/pod-product-compliance
Lightning Source LLC
Chambersburg PA
CBHW050612160726
48003CB00003B/1149